ANIMALS!

by harrop

for animal rescuers everywhere

ISBN-13: 978-1548717186

...from the beginning: Powell River News 1966,
followed later by a spot in The Vancouver Sun....

Then came the BackBench years, in The Globe and Mail.
Thank you, Warren.....

CAT'S TO-DO LIST
TIE DOG'S TAIL IN KNOT
PHONE 'MR. SUSHI' - ORDER IN
REPORT VET TO BETTER BUSINESS BUREAU.
grahamharrop

A RODENT TALKS
grahamharrop.com 3-7
'YEAR OF THE RAT' MY FOOT! I'VE CHECKED AND THERE ARE NO PARADES PLANNED!
I WENT DOWN TO THE CITY DUMP AND THERE'S NOT A SINGLE SIGN SAYING 'CONGRATS'!
NO-IT'LL BE A YEAR LIKE ALL YEARS - JUST ME, SOME BRIE AND A BOTTLE OF MOUSCATEL!

NoVeMBeR 9 2022

Despite five years behind bars, Carl, a small Norwich canary, is denied parole - correction officials considering him a flight risk.

grahamharrop.coM 5-26

ANIMALS AT THE OLYMPICS

THE TEDDY BEARS' PICNIC
THE TRUTH COMES OUT!

Long thought of as idyllic, the Teddy Bears' Picnic was in fact a drunken brawl, spurred on by a series of insults such as 'salmon breath', 'berry butt' and 'hey! - carpet fur!'

harrop 10-22

JUST AS LYLE WAS ABOUT TO GIVE UP ON EVER SEEING A WHALE OFF THE EAST COAST, A STRANGE AND MIRACULOUS THING HAPPENED.

HARPeR's CAT

Continue to work on memoirs. Am hoping to reveal the hell of the last five years here at 24 Sussex and how the Harper regime has affected me.

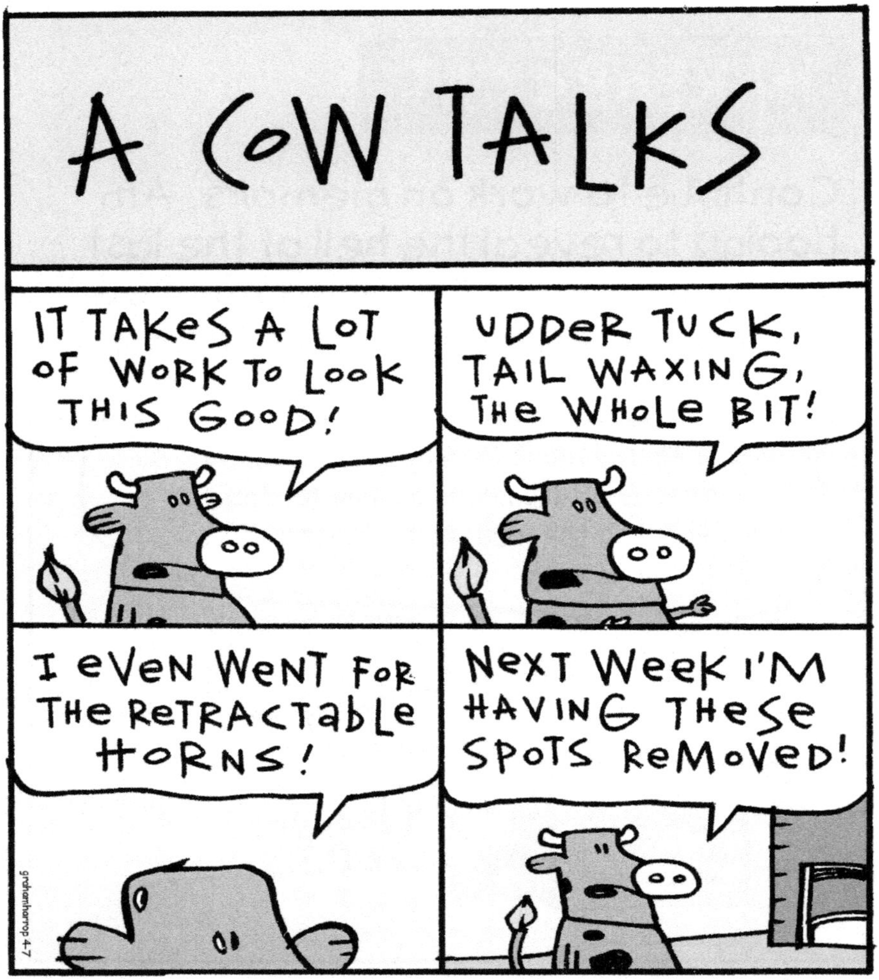
A COW TALKS
IT TAKES A LOT OF WORK TO LOOK THIS GOOD!
UDDER TUCK, TAIL WAXING, THE WHOLE BIT!
I EVEN WENT FOR THE RETRACTABLE HORNS!
NEXT WEEK I'M HAVING THESE SPOTS REMOVED!
grahamharrop 4-7

ATTEND PERFORMANCE OF 'CATS' — STAND UP — BOO.
LIE DOWN AT LEAST ONCE WITHOUT TURNING AROUND.
WRITE LETTER TO POSTAL WORKERS - APOLOGIZE.
DOGS' BUCKET LIST.
grahamharrop.com 7-16

RACOON
NOTEPAD

'NO LID TOO TIGHT!'

Lew -
they fingered Zeb for the Wilkey's
can. I told him - 'Don't take off the
mask - don't take off the mask!'
But did he listen?? N-o-o-o-o-o.
Anyway - the 8:15 job at the
Henderson's is off!
Lookin' cute ain't gonna save us
this time!
              BoB.

I DON'T KNOW WHY EVERYONE SKATES ON THE RIDEAU CANAL IN THE WINTER!
IT'S A LOT LESS CROWDED IN THE SUMMER!
GRAHAMHARROP.COM 12-24

Why Bees Get Mad

A FIELD MOUSE TALKS

A TORTOISE CONFESSES

THAT RACE WITH THE HARE WAS FIXED!

I SPIKED HIS CARROT JUICE WITH SOMINEX.

THERE SHOULD HAVE BEEN A DRUG TEST!

DID YOU REALLY THINK A TORTOISE COULD BEAT A HARE?

TWO MOSQUITOES TALK

IT'S OKAY FOR YOU TO GIVE *PINTS* TO THE bLOOD bank!

Yeah!

ALL *WE* ASK IS A SMIDGEN — ONE TINY, LITTLE Drop!

Yeah!

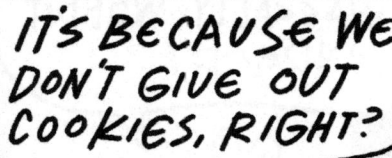

YOU DON'T EVEN HAVE TO Go *DOWNTOWN* FOR PETE'S SAKE!

Yeah!

IT'S BECAUSE WE DON'T GIVE OUT COOKIES, RIGHT?

Yeah!

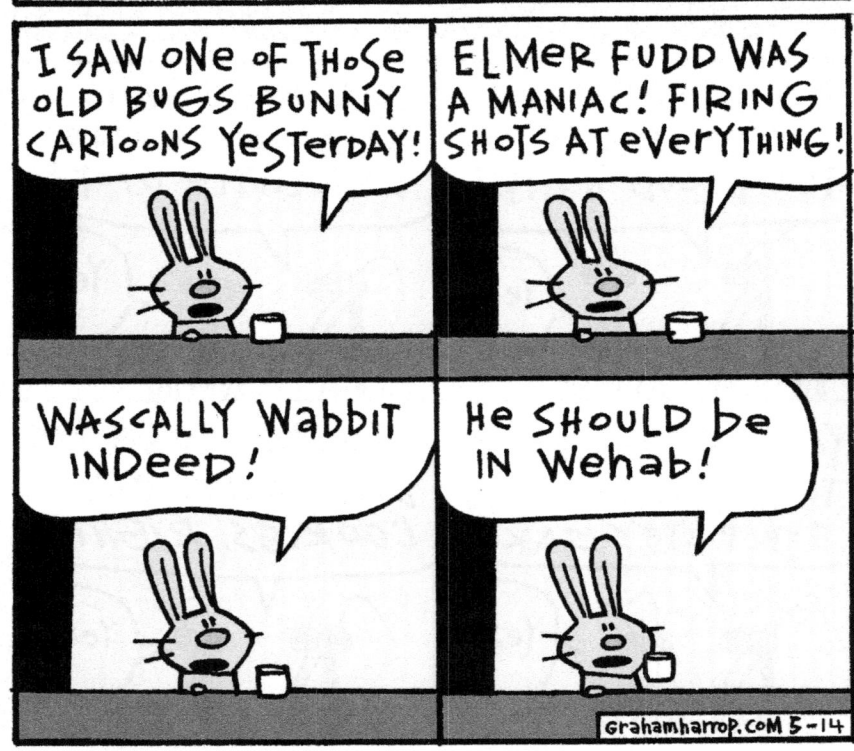

Ten seconds with Margaret Atwood

THE MAIN REASON WHY BIRDS NEST IN MAILBOXES

A MOMENT WITH THE PINE BEETLES
OKAY- EVERYBODY STOP CHEWING!
STOP YOUR MUNCHING- IT'S TIME FOR LUNCH!
DO WE HAVE A GREAT UNION OR WHAT?
grahamharrop.com 3-8

CATS TALK ABOUT LOSING WEIGHT

THEY SAY A CAT SHOULD ONLY BE AS WIDE AS HIS WHISKERS... I'M GOING TO HAVE TO STRETCH MINE!

I'D SIGN UP FOR 'THE BIGGEST LOSER' IF IT WAS HOSTED BY A MOUSE!

AS SOON AS THE SCALE IS FIXED, I'M GOING TO TRY WEIGH MYSELF AGAIN!

2-11 Grahamharrop.com

IN A BRITISH COLUMBIA FOREST

CATS AT THE OLYMPICS

IT WOULD BE THE LAST TIME THAT THE OAK BAY BIRDWATCHING CLUB WOULD VENTURE OUT INTO THE WOODS WITHOUT A PRIOR PHONE CALL.

Muskrats talk at night

A couple of muskrats talk

HARD TO FATHOM!

The NUMBER oNe NAMe FoR GeckoS iN CANADA is <u>MERLe!</u>

INTeReSTiNGLY. GORDON WAS THe ALL-TiMe MoST PoPULAR UNTiL THe MoVie **WALL STREET!**

Grahamharrop.coM 12-3

IT HAPPeNeD oN chriSTMas EVe

SUDDENLY REALIZING THAT REINDEER CAN'T FLY, IT WAS A PIVOTAL, TELLING MOMENT FOR RUDOLPH AND THE EIGHT DINERS BELOW AT TOBBLINO'S RESTAURANT IN YORKVILLE.

Graham harrop. co 12-24

AT A PINE BEETLE CONCERT

A CANADIAN ELK REMINISCES

I came <u>this</u> close to being the face of the Canadian quarter!

They invited me back to Ottawa to meet with the board of the Mint.

They said: 'Let's meet for lunch and discuss your possible tender.'

As soon as I heard the words 'lunch' and 'tender' I was gone!

grahamharrop.com 6-16

TWO BEDBUGS AFTER A TRYST

Two Fleas in a Bar

MICE IN THE COMMONS

IT OCCURRED TO NORMAN THAT HE WAS
USING FAR, FAR TOO MUCH SALT.

I DON'T CARE **HOW** BRISTLY PINE NEEDLES ARE ...FIND YOUR OWN BED!

WELL, IT HAS HAPPENED. I AM
LAST FISH IN SEA. ED'S GONE.
MERV'S GONE. OLD COUPLE FROM
THE NORTH SHOAL HAVE GONE.
STOOPID PEOPLE OVER-FISHING!
AND JUST WHEN I LEARNED TO
WRITE WITH PEN AND PAPER.

FISH
DIARY
2048

I'LL ONLY EAT HERRING FOR BREAKFAST.
WELL, I'VE LOST OVER 30 POUNDS THIS YEAR!
I'M VACATIONING IN MEXICO COME JULY.
iPODS
WWW.GRAHAMHARROP.COM 4-7

Faced with the threat of a discrimination suit, Ed chose to hire Harold and hope for the best.

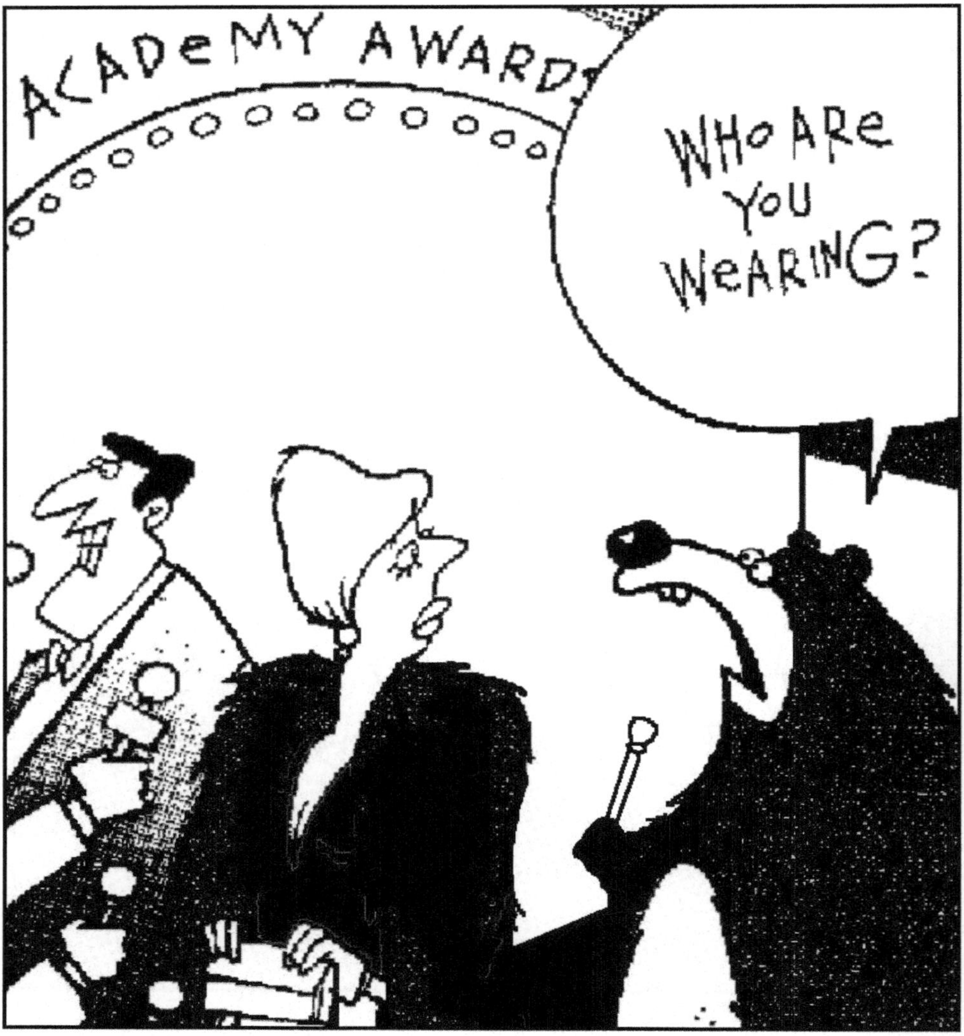
ACADEMY AWARDS
WHO ARE YOU WEARING?

AND HOW ABOUT THOSE BATTERY CAGES? THEY PACK YOU IN TIGHTER THAN AIR CANADA. I SHOULDA BEEN BORN A RHINO. TRY TO STACK THEM ON TOP OF EACH OTHER AND YOU DON'T SIT DOWN FOR A WEEK! AND HEY! — IF I LAY AN EGG HERE, AT LEAST I GET A REACTION!
WWW.GRAHAMHARROP.COM 4-15
CHICKEN COMEDIANS

...AND I STAND CONVINCED THAT THIS IS ONE OF THE BEST MOVIES OF THE YEAR SO I'M GIVING IT A BIG THUMBS UP ... OH, G!!*$!!
WWW.GRAHAMHARROP.COM 7-12
WHY SNAKES MAKE POOR MOVIE CRITICS

ONLY ALAN WAS PREPARED TO ACKNOWLEDGE THE ELEPHANT IN THE ROOM.

POLICE BLOTTER
WWW.GRAHAMHARROP.COM 12-6
ALTHOUGH POLICE DOGS ARE AN INTEGRAL PART OF POLICE WORK AND OF GREAT HELP IN CATCHING CROOKS, CATS REFUSE TO GO INTO THE PROFESSION... SAYING THAT THE BULLETPROOF VESTS MAKE THEM LOOK TAWDRY AND CHEAP!
POLICE

INTERVIEW WITH A CANADA Goose

grahamharrop.coM 2-10

WHY DO WE FLY IN A 'V'? NO SECRET- IT'S USUALLY THE INITIAL OF THE LEAD GOOSE.

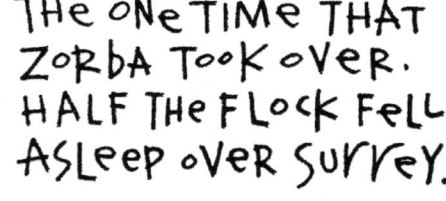

VICTOR, VINCENT VANCE, VIOLET, VELMA, VITO — WE GET THERE IN NO TIME

THE ONE TIME THAT ZORBA TOOK OVER. HALF THE FLOCK FELL ASLEEP OVER SURREY.

FREDDY GAVE ME A DIAMOND FLEA COLLAR FOR CHRISTMAS, BUT I HAD TO THROW IT AWAY AFTER A FEW MONTHS!
harrop 3-1 WWW.GRAHAMHARROP.COM

Debate With The Fisheries Minister
grahamharrop.com 3-19
There's nothing wrong with the seal hunt.
You're not the one getting bonked on the head!
The seal hunt is humane.
No humans were hurt during the whole thing!!
Look - let's discuss this over lunch.
Flipper pie come to mind?

HEY! ARE YOU HOUSE TRAINED YET?
WHAT'S WITH THE DOG COLLAR?
C'MON! JUST ONE PHOTO!
WWW.GRAHAMHARROP.COM 4-25
PUPARAZZI

6-30 WWW.GRAHAMHARROP.COM
SORRY—I MADE A LITTLE MESS ON THE STAIRWELL BACK THERE...!
G
IT WAS THE LAST TIME ED USED GREYHOUND COURIERS

Printed in Great Britain
by Amazon